Gianna Patriarca

DAUGHTERS FOR SALE

Poetry and Prose

D1636065

Guernica

Toronto/New York/Lancaster
1997

Antonio D'Alfonso, editor
Guernica Editions Inc.
P.O. Box 117, Station P, Toronto (ON), Canada M5S 2S6
250 Sonwil Drive, Buffalo, N.Y. 14225-5516 U.S.A.
Gazelle, Falcon House, Queen Square, Lancaster LA1 1RN U.K.

The Publisher gratefully acknowledges support from
The Canada Council and Ontario Arts Council.
'Espresso, Camaros and Gianni Morandi' was written as an oral
presentation for a symposium entitled 'Out of the House' and
later published in *The Eyetalian*. 'Perfect Love' was previously
published in the League of Canadian Poets Newsletter in 1995.

Typeset by Faye Martin, Toronto.
Printed in Canada.
Legal Deposit — First Quarter
National Library of Canada
Library of Congress Card Number: 96-78721.

Contents

Acknowledgments

Thank you to my publisher Antonio D'Alfonso and to Guernica for their support and determination. To all my friends whose love and laughter make all things possible and to my family who keep my heart beating.

To the memory of my friend,
Marisa Fiaschetti-Pittelli.
The party is over too soon
that's why we always stayed
for the last dance. I miss you.

We were just ordinary people trying to make sense of our lives, and for that I thank my grandparents. I'm lucky that I had the sense to listen and the heart to care.

Nikki Giovanni

Espresso, Camaros and Gianni Morandi

The most vivid memory I have of leaving my home town Ceprano, in the region of Lazio, in 1960, with my mother and sister to join my father who had emigrated five years earlier (like many other families at the time), is that of my two elderly grandparents standing beneath the enormous oak tree that stood in front of our small country house. A small, stone, four room house whose pale blue stucco walls were faded by the burning sun that made the house blend with the sky. The long pathway to the door lined with great rosemary bushes and tall purple iris.

A dozen or so people were gathered beneath the shade of the oak to wish us a safe journey and to embrace us for the last time. My aunts and uncle, cousins and friends busily shook hands and handed my mother envelopes to be delivered to family members in the new land.

The June air was suffocating. My unsuspecting baby sister chased the chickens, unconcerned. Tears and sweat were one salty mixture as I kissed each waiting cheek in the crowd. Then I stood in front of them. My tall, thin stoic grandmother, with clenched fists and trembling lips, tried with all her might not to cry. My very gentle, rotund grandfather, leaned on his home-made wooden cane. His one free hand quivered as it reached out for me. His eyes, red, moist and incredibly sad.

I locked my arms around his knees, like a trap, and held on tight. I would not let go, I could not let go, screaming like a wild thing until I felt my small lungs explode as my heart climbed towards my throat. At that very moment, while my uncle and mother tried to tear me away, kicking and screaming, from my grandfather's knees, I knew I had no choice. The decision had been made for me. The choices would go on being made for me for a long time to come.

We arrived in Canada the 'promised land.' We came in pursuit of a dream. A dream of a better life, a richer life, a life of freedom. We learned too quickly that dreams often become nightmares.

I began my new life in the basement of a tall, dark house that reminded me of the cemetery mausoleums in Italy. Many of us at the time began our lives in the basements, cellars of these constructions. Basements we had never known in Italy. It was as if we had walked from light into the darkness of a dungeon. This dungeon represented our new life: we were hidden, tucked away, buried alive. We often lived two or three families in one house. Usually the families were related, brothers, sisters, aunts and uncles, cousins, or sometimes *paesani*.

Our parents disappeared almost instantly into the world of factories. They left in the early dark morning and returned in the late dark evening, and walked into the dark, damp, musty basements they called home.

At age ten, I became the surrogate mother to my younger sister. I became an adequate homemaker. I cleaned, learned to cook. I washed and ironed clothes and often had a simple dinner prepared when my parents returned from their jobs. Toys and dolls, little ceramic tea sets, games and skipping ropes had become quickly a memory. Childhood became a fading photograph hanging slightly off-center on grandma's kitchen wall.

We entered public school in the neighborhood of Danforth and Woodbine where the only Italian-immigrant students were my sister, two of our cousins and myself. There were no ESL classes. They put us back a year thinking that, because we could not speak the language, we must also be slow-learners. We fooled them. We learned the language quickly and this helped us survive. Our names became Canadianized, Concetta became Connie, Assunta became Susan, Salvatore became Sam. I was called Joanne. It would be decades later when I finally reclaimed my name.

In the 1960s there was an invasion of all things British: The Beatles, Mary Quant, Jean Shrimpton, Marianne Faithful, Carnaby Street. The Hippy Revolution was in full swing. Drugs, freedom of expression, sex and rock and roll. Well all of this might as well have been happening on Mars. It was so far removed from my life and the lives of my immigrant friends at the time. We experienced only through black and white television what was happening in the world outside our community.

We did not have the luxury of becoming hippies. We were much too busy being mothers to our siblings, busy little homemakers and students who often held part-time jobs in local grocery stores, variety stores and bakeries. In the summer during school breaks our parents took us into the factories for our holidays. We always handed our money over to our parents without question and were given a few dollars for our effort, often used for bus fare to our jobs. We accepted things as they were, we believed and embraced our situation without challenge. We were part of a family. We helped each other.

We supported each other. We were on our way to making things better.

Growing into young women we were made to believe we had roughly three choices for our future. The first choice was going to a commercial high school and learning the skills to become a good secretary. The second choice (if we were pretty enough) was to get married before or after graduation, and become good wives and mothers. The third choice (if we were slightly more ambitious) was to become school teachers or bank tellers. We bought into these role models without question. And although there was nothing wrong with these choices we were convinced there were no other options.

Our social lives were pretty much centered around the activities our parents exposed us to. Weddings and home-town feasts, being the two most vivid events.

Weekend visits to relatives, friends and *paesani,* Sunday afternoon picnics at the local park, a day in Niagara Falls. At all of these events our parents and relatives kept a discreet eye open for perspective husbands for us.

Some of us dared to step over the line just a little bit during our late teen years. There were activities we practiced in secret: the Sunday afternoon dances at the Piper Club on Dufferin Street, The Rotonda Hall, the Brandon Club and the Isabella. These dark, unsophisticated, sometime run-down places were for us a dangerous adventure, provocation to sin. Girlfriends would meet and quickly make their way to the washrooms to apply the forbidden eye shadows and lipsticks. Hair spray clouded the whole interior of the girls' washroom. In these afternoon clubs we would make contact with the young Italian men and boys and dance the afternoon away to popular songs of artists from Italy. We managed to experience limited sex in red Firebirds and Camaros and the occasional Fiat but always went home intact and before dark.

The St. Clair Theater and the Pylon Theater of College Street (both no longer there) pre-date the Columbus Center and were for us almost cultural centers because it was in these two theaters that we could watch Italian films, listen to Italian songs and see the wonderful images of the country we had left behind. Italian films were the one visible reminder of our Italian culture. We went to the movies a lot. Saturday nights and Sunday afternoons

12

these theaters were full of Italian families, young, old, middle-aged and infants. We all sat there devouring the beautiful, romantic Italy we had left behind. For two hours we thought we reclaimed our culture. A culture of art, music, good food, ocean and sunshine. Such innocence. The films were unbelievably mediocre but to us they were works of art. I sat with my girlfriends, dreaming, while watching stars like Massimo Ranieri and Gianni Morandi romance and sing to the dark-eyed Italian beauties on the screen. I believed if only I could fall in love with a man like Gianni or Massimo all my dreams would come true. The dream was often interrupted by the intruding leg of a man sitting beside me trying hard to rub his body against mine. And although the desire to punch this intruder in the face was always there rarely did I or my girlfriends do it. We were passive. We would stand up and move seats. We understood that men behaved this way and it was part of what we had to endure and accept. It never felt right. It felt humiliating. I knew in my heart I should have reacted.

As girlfriends we spent much of our spare time in each other's homes, usually in the basements drinking espresso, sneaking cigarettes, exploring new feelings and talking about boys and marriage. We wanted sex (the little we knew about sex) but we didn't dare. We were virgins, well, not completely. Whatever we did we lied about it. We had been taught fear like a prayer.

Fear governed whatever we did. It kept us in line. The fear of getting pregnant, of being defined *puttane*, of thinking thoughts that were sinful, of not meeting the ideals of our parents. Because of fear and guilt we communicated little to our parents about what was deep in our hearts. We had no role models, no one but ourselves to talk to and this created a lasting bond among us. We had wonderful times together, innocent times that created friendships which have lasted for decades.

The only other person in the community we had to talk to was the priest. We never told him the truth about anything.

We lived in a very close community who was tied to the values and traditions of their region in Italy. Our religion and our language united us.

There was no Yorkdale or Columbus Center. Armani and Versace were still young boys probably playing with themselves. Style was something our mothers and aunts created for us on their old Singer sewing machines. We didn't discover Germaine Greer or Gloria Steinam until we were mothers ourselves. We felt very isolated in our communities. As young women we craved a role model besides our mothers. After all the men had Johnny Lombardi, the family had Johnny Lombardi, the business men had Johnny Lombardi, we had no one.

Because our experiences are all unique it would be presumptuous of me to speak for a whole generation of Italian-Canadian women who grew up in Toronto in the 1960s and 1970s. The responsibility of a collective voice is much too heavy a burden to carry. A writer can only speak for herself and hopefully in writing that voice others can recognize the melodies of their own songs. In any language.

Daughters for Sale

ROSARIA

You want to listen to my story

how polite you are

but it will not make a difference

you will laugh a little
a little you will cry
it will not change anything
tears and laughter change nothing
i have done both
many times, even when i *believed*
i am not a dreamer anymore

sit
i will tell you my story
because you say you want to hear it
but do not judge everything by me
stories are all i have left

i was born far from this perfect garden
of cement and wrought iron
i was born a fish in a Calabrian sea
i cannot remember the name

it was a Greek name
on the other side was Sicily

touch my skin
feel how rough, dry, like salt
sometimes i can taste my skin
it smells of the sea
i lift my face to feel the sun
i remember the way it walked on my flesh
warm like an angel and sometimes with the
fiery steps of the devil

in this garden the sun wears shoes

i came here long ago
before your mother thought of you
it was a little after Mussolini took
my mother's wedding ring and my brother
his dead body in her arms
his blood on the stones of the piazza
the church bells screaming
my father went crazy
He just walked about talking
talking to my brother
talking to the empty spot at the table
talking to the fields, to the fireplace
talking to himself until his own tongue dropped
not long after i married a man
from a photograph
a photograph sent from across the ocean
i married a man i recognized only
from the waist up
a man in an envelope

i prayed he had legs

this man was our passport
our ticket to paradise
i did not know about paradise
was it farther than Naples?

the man had legs and he had arms
he gave me bread i gave him children
he had very large hands
but not large enough to touch me

my man is gone
and my children are busy
so i sit here by this fountain
with all this wool in my hands
and i knit

what do you think they will do
with all my knitting?

My Morning Child

You sleep
curled inside my arm
your head has stopped
my blood rushing
but i will not move

your breathing
is the only sound
in the white bone
of this room

you will never see
how beautiful you are
in the morning light
how the sun
finds its way
through the skylight
and webs its rays
in your angel pasta hair
your tiny moist lips
teasing my breast

where did you come from,
you perfect small thing?

you move
and i turn to stone
i will not disturb this moment
you, safe in the folds of my skin

don't awaken too soon, my darling girl
the world can wait

Painted Windows

Mamma is crying in her room downstairs. I hear mamma crying every night since we got here in this dark, tall house with all these stairs. This starved house with windows painted shut. Windows that keep the air out. This house with wooden floors she makes me scrub over and over with bleach and turpentine. She says she likes the smell. She says it's a clean smell. It makes my hands burn and my skin peel. Mamma isn't worried. She shows me her hands. I guess she knows best.

I hate this house. This house on this street where all the women look like my mother. Where all the houses look like each other. I hate the darkness of this house, especially at night. The nights when all I hear is mamma crying. The nights I can't breathe and want to break all the windows. I'm not sure why mamma cries. I think she misses nonno and nonna, like I do. Maybe she cries for them. My father is never home. Maybe she cries for him.

My sister Nina is six, but she looks older. Except when she sleeps. She looks like a little baby. I watch her sometimes. Her eyes perfectly still. Her long soft lashes resting on her cheeks. A doll by her side, safe and warm. I watch her little body quiver and rise. I listen to her sighs. I watch for a long time and then I hear mamma's tears crashing into her pillow like broken glass.

I want to walk down the stairs, open the door, run into her arms, jump into her bed. I want to stop the sadness, sweep up the tears. Make everything clean. Make it all smell nice. But somehow I can't. I don't know why. So I listen. Counting all the tears. The last one. Silence. I fall asleep.

On Sunday mamma put on a blue dress and red lipstick. She'd bought Nina and me new shoes. We put them on and danced round and round, tap tapping on the wooden floors. Mamma packed a shopping bag with sandwiches. She took us to High Park to walk in the grass and to look at the flowers. She took us to sit by the pond and eat our sandwiches and throw bits of bread to the ducks. I liked High Park. Liked the long streetcar ride. Liked watching the city move through the streetcar windows. Watching the sun play hide and seek with the buildings. We counted the traffic lights. Happy little girls in new shiny shoes, hand in hand, with a pretty, smiling mother in bright red lipstick.

Three traffic lights before the park. The houses begin to change from small plain ones to beautiful large ones. They look like castles. Flowers all around, windows with colored glass. Open windows. Big, open windows. 'I want to live there! That one, no, that one, I want to live in that one.'

They're yelling again. My father's fists hard on the kitchen table. Over and over. The words in Italian that make my mother scream. Nina and I huddle together in the same bed. Confused. Scared. The slaps echo through the house. They don't stop. Mamma's body against the furniture. We start to cry and hold each other tight. Nobody hears us.

Mamma left for work at six. Papa didn't come home at all. Got to get Nina ready. Get myself ready and go to school. I'm cold. I want mamma, I want nonna. I want somebody.

Nina burned herself today, poured boiling water all over her leg. I was cooking pasta for our lunch. She screamed and I screamed too. No one was home. I put her in the bathtub and ran cold water over her leg. The skin looked funny. Nina screamed louder. I phoned my aunt. 'Butter,' she said. 'Put butter on it.' It didn't seem right. I kept running the cold water. Held her hand tight. Kept kissing her wet cheeks over and over. We cried for a long time, alone in the bathroom. The doctor said I did the right thing. I was a smart, quick thinking girl. I got hit anyway. Should have been more careful. The scar will stay. Mamma was grateful it wasn't Nina's face. Nina has a beautiful face.

Got my period today. It feels awful. Mamma made me stay in bed. Said I could skip school. She didn't explain anything. 'Just stay in bed.' She came back a little later holding something in her hand. Thick cotton pieces of material folded into a long strip. She told me to pin them to my panties with safety pins. Diapers! They looked like diapers. 'I don't want to wear them, I don't want to!' I screamed at her. She looked at me with the saddest eyes I had ever seen. She walked out of the room without saying a word. Left me there with the diapers in my hand. I sat on my bed squeezing the safety pins open and shut.

My first Christmas in Canada. I love the little colored lights that shine everywhere in the city. I have never seen so many lights, so many colors that flicker and wink like magic fireflies in winter. They make me feel happy. I stare out the window watching the tall, dark houses all lit with these magic lights. The pine trees in the front garden, the verandas, the dry, naked bushes all alive with colored lights. I want lights. I beg mamma for lights for our window. The one that never opens. But there's no money for lights. No money for unnecessary things. I stare out the window wishing I lived in another house.

My aunt and uncle came on Christmas Eve. They have five sons. They were all born here. Nina and I don't speak English well, they make no effort to understand us. They're boys, they don't really care about us. They play by themselves.

Mamma cooked fish. Only fish on Christmas Eve. *Baccalà* in tomato sauce, onions and raisins. Lots of onions and some black olives, just like nonna used to make. Papa likes to help at Christmas and he made spaghetti with anchovies, garlic and chopped parsley. My uncle Ettore brought wine. His own home made wine. Says he can only drink his own. He knows what's in it. He poured some for all of us. The children got half a glass. His boys added ginger ale to fill up the glass. Nina and I drank it without ginger ale. After the wine and the food we all felt good. We laughed and my uncle told stories. He told them in Italian and his boys looked bored but Nina and I laughed till our sides hurt. I saw my father put his arm around my mother. She got up and went to the kitchen to make coffee.

My aunt and uncle left just after midnight. My father left a little while after them. He came back two days later.

It's January. The lights still shine in the city but they do not seem to have the same magic. I feel they will soon begin to die and disappear. I will miss them. My nose against the frozen window watching the growing darkness. The days are so cold. I can't get warm. I can't get Nina up in the morning. She cries for mamma. Mamma's at the factory. Nina doesn't care about my explanation. She keeps crying. I feed her cheerios and milk. I dress her up. I comb and braid her hair. She wants mamma. I start to get angry. I shake her. She cries even louder. Buries her little head in the hood of her jacket. 'I want mamma!' she yells. Then she wraps her arms around my waist.

Mamma got a telegram today. Nonno died. She fell on the floor, screaming and tearing at her clothes. I tried to pick her up. Nina was trembling and crying out:

24

'Mommy, mommy, mommy.' Mamma put her arms around us and sobbed in big gulps. I could feel her chest against my face, it was warm, wet and pounding so fast. All of a sudden she pushes me away and holds onto Nina. I walk around the rooms, trying to think of what to do. Papa isn't home. I don't know where he is. I don't know when he will come home. I call my aunt. Soon relatives start to appear at the door. They bring food. They bring coffee and baked cookies. They talk in whispers. My mother sits in the corner of the couch. The relatives take turns comforting her. They put their arms around her and try to feed her. She refuses. She just keeps wailing. My relatives move around the small rooms in careful steps. There is nowhere to go. It's as if we are playing a game. Smiling, walking, bumping into each other.

Everyone left very late. My aunt is staying over. My mother hasn't moved from the corner of the couch. My aunt is washing dishes. Nina is asleep. Papa finally came home. He said nothing. He is standing by the window a beer in one hand and a cigarette in the other. They don't look at each other. They seem so far away. I feel so far away. I wonder what they are thinking. I squeeze my eyes and they become blurry. I imagine them in each other's arms. I imagine their faces close together, their cheeks touching. I watch for such a long time squeezing and opening my eyes, but they never move. I hide in the dark by the stairs. I do not move. We are all like the windows of this dark, tall house. Windows that won't open.

Birthday Poem

ROSINA

Rosi is forty-three
and flying to the Orient
we have come to celebrate
her birthday and her new adventure
we have come with wine and cigarettes
and a big chocolate cake
fourteen of us
all shapes, all sizes
mostly large
mostly dark-eyed
mostly Italian
except for Sally and Bonita
but they are one of us
we are home with each other
there is the one story
we are immigrant girls from the 1960s
the in-between women who fit
nowhere very comfortably
but we are home with each other
with the sound of our laughter
and with our incredible need to discover
the Orient

My Husband

Sometimes i think
my husband is a saint
he allowed himself to be
re-baptized just to marry me
he let the priest do that
holy water thing all over
his New Zealand-Scottish head
he became a Catholic just to marry me
took those sacred vows
wore a suit and tie
and danced with my aunts
just for me
the girl with the wrong package
the most unlikely débutante
but my husband is a silent saint
polite and discreet
unlike the saints i grew up with
who held their eyes in their hands
and paraded their open wounds
bled openly for admiration
he is a saint of understatement
a sort of socialist saint
who carries his heart
not on his sleeve but
neatly tucked into his
breast pocket, keeping mine company

The Last Confession

PEPPINA

The only real sin
is being born

my son sits
in quiet duty
at the foot of
my hospital bed
he has not removed his coat
he is not sure
whether to go or to stay
his legs are uncrossed

he took the day off work
to bring me here
his wife did not come
she did not want to lose a day's pay
i understand
the value of a day's pay

my son is not my child anymore
he cannot comfort me
i cannot comfort him
the years have changed our position
they say
that is the way it should be

my daughter will come soon
to relieve him

he will go without guilt
i must look presentable
because my children care

my daughter will comb my hair
and pass a wet face cloth
over my eyes and body
she will force me to powder my skin
she will rub cream on my brittle hands
my daughter will straighten my bed
make sure i eat everything on my plastic tray
she will insist i walk
so my blood will travel
to the parts of me i no longer feel

my body wants to rest
my body wants to lie flat
my arms want to fold over my sunken chest
and my eyes, my eyes want to lose themselves
deep into what they have left of memories

my children do not want me to die
death is too final
like the dark after a sunset
it interrupts everything

my daughter tells me there will be visitors
so i must wear my best nightgown
i do not need visitors
what to say to visitors about my pain
pray with me, eat an orange

will they understand
i do not have my language anymore
will they recognize me

the fourth bed in this room
the old quiet woman
in the corner, by the window
a box of fine imported chocolates
on the night table

Carmela's Man

Carmela's man decided to stop living the day his only son married a Canadian divorcée with two teenage children she had had by two different men. Carmela's man put all his hopes in this one son since he had married his eldest daughter to a Greek electrician. Besides, he pretty much disowned his middle daughter who had left home to live with a woman who wore a gold earring in her nose. Carmela's man hoped with all his heart that this one son would do the right thing. Whatever the right thing was. It didn't matter to him that this one son was born in Canada in 1960, that he had grown up in Windsor, Ontario, and enjoyed Canadian things, such as hockey and beer. No, he never considered that maybe the possibility of his son marrying a Canadian woman wasn't all that strange or improbable.

Carmela's man was an honorable patriarch. He was a hard working immigrant man, and a family man with Christian values and a good appetite. He had labored hard all his life and done plenty of overtime at the auto plant. He also spent the occasional weekends working at Nasone's body shop and got paid cash. Now he owned an eight room house on a half acre of land with a grapevine that harvested enough white grapes to make two full demijohns of wine every late September.

There were two pear trees and one plum tree on the property and a two-car garage with an automatic door opener. The four door yellow Le Sabre had only traveled thirty thousand kilometers and shined like new. These treasures would one day belong to his son... If his son did the right thing. Carmela's man hadn't worked so hard, sweated blood for so long just to leave his treasures to some Canadian divorcée with two bastard children, who just happened to have gotten her hooks into his unsus-pecting son.

The day Carmela's man stopped talking was the day his son announced his engagement to the woman Car-mela referred to as the Canadian whore, that was also the day Carmela began the novenas. She recited nine prayers each day for a total of nine days. These novenas were to help her son see the light. Whatever the light was. But in between the prayers she cursed. She cursed and prayed and prayed and cursed. She cursed the day they had come to this land. She cursed the day her children grew up. She cursed her man's silence. It never once occurred to her that her man might have stopped talking because he sim-ply had nothing more to say. None of his children had ever really listened to him. Oh, they had made polite motions out or respect and duty and love but they had always, in the end, made their own decisions, their own choices. Carmela never considered that perhaps this was the way it should have been.

The Canadian whore was really not such a bad girl. It's true she had been around a couple of blocks, and more than likely a piazza or two, but she was a gentle sort who rarely spoke. It is also true that her teeth were all replaced, her eyes a little too close together and her hair orange. Her round breasts, however, were firm and her stomach flat, unlike any of the women in Carmela's fam-ily. Indeed her teenage children were a little wild and had dirty mouths, but that was not so different from any other teenager. She was not a very good cook but she did open cans quickly and knew how to work all the buttons on the microwave. And she did keep a clean house. Dur-ing her leisure time she enjoyed hooking rugs. A horse's head rug, two by one meter large, hung proudly on her lavender living room wall. It was the first thing you saw when you walked into the front door of her modest insul-brick bungalow. Of course Carmela and her man had never seen the rug because they could not bear to set foot in the house their son shared with this shameless, unacceptable whore.

The day the Canadian whore gave birth to their grandson was the day Carmela's man stopped walking. Like a miracle he was paralyzed. His legs and bones grew soft and fleshy. Carmela's curses and prayers became more frequent and loud. The fact that the baby was a healthy, beautiful boy, who weighed three and a half kilograms and had his daddy's fine looks and normal eyes, didn't seem to matter at all.

The first time Carmela and her man saw the baby was when he was three weeks old. His daddy had brought him over to meet his grandparents. They stared at him for a while until Carmela finally took him into her arms and immediately made the sign of the cross over his tiny forehead. She then gently placed a folded, white linen handkerchief that contained a spoonful of salt into the baby's shirt. She mumbled a few words and made another sign of the cross. This was to protect the newborn from any evil the wicked world might have in store for him. She handed the baby back to her son and asked what they had named him. 'Saverino, like papa,' answered her son. That was the day Carmela's man developed breathing problems and they had to rush him to the hospital.

Intensive care was a new foreign place for Carmela and her man. People lay motionless, connected to tubes, wires, little television screens. Carmela's man was silent, a plastic mask over his face. He seemed peaceful enough. Carmela sat next to him fondling the beads in her hands. She began her litany of prayers and curses keeping her voice low and muffled. She cursed the day she gave birth to her children. She cursed the Canadian whore and her bastards. Then she prayed for them all.

Carmela's eyes were open when they found her but her pale lips were uncharacteristically shut. The beads in a knot around her forefinger. Carmela had never once considered that maybe there was a natural order to things, people, places. Things just took their inevitable course.

Her man's breathing got better. And although he never spoke he slept soundly for six more years. Slept on a corduroy couch directly opposite the horse's head on the lavender wall in the living room of the Canadian whore's insul-brick bungalow.

A Kiss

She had not kissed
any other man
but her husband since
she promised
the Catholic Church
she would not

that was decades ago
she broke that promise
one summer night
when the moon was full
and her heart unsettled

the shape of another's lips
on her trembling mouth
the sloping of a different nose
that rested on her cheek
the elated scent of a new face
and the strange feeling inside
of something forbidden

she sometimes thought
of forbidden things
but had always shaken
such thoughts away
trying to jumble them in her mind
she dealt the same way with her fantasies

allowing them a conception
but never a birth
as if life were a
mortal sin

Her Son

CELESTINA

I watched her fuss over him
as if he were a prince
an angel
a divine gift from God
her golden child
with the clear glass eyes
and natural curls
a perfect little man
with perfect little parts

and when he grew
i watched her caress his shirts
with her bent fingers
as she ironed out each crease
erasing any evidence of imperfection
i watched her fold each one
into a perfect square
buttoned to the neck
then she'd straighten the chest of drawers
and gently lay each piece of clothing
as if it were blessed
with such care and concentration
like the women in church who arrange the altar
i watched her prepare his lunch
the sandwiches always moist
the fruit always unbruised
and always something she had baked
for his male sweet tooth

i watched her slip twenty-dollar bills
into his trouser pockets
just in case
and when he allowed her
she would caress his strong cheek
bello mio, she would say
and then she'd place her fingers
on her lips as if she had let slip
some deep secret

she would look at him
and nothing else mattered
he could do no wrong

i watched her stare out
into a thousand midnights
waiting like a soft shadow
pinned to her lace curtains
waiting, for the lights of his car
to silence her heart
his footsteps up the walk
his key in the door
and then she would breathe
and disappear

i watched her love him
without fatigue
without expectations
then i would go
and iron my own clothes

Barolo, Piemonte

Carmelo and Andrew
are tasting wines
all afternoon
with the magic bottles
of the region
more precious than jewels
labels that are works of art
i cannot drink as much
so i wait in the gardens
drinking in the azure of the sky
the color the Virgin Mother would wear
laced with thin, silk clouds

the afternoon is still
and the doves coo beneath
the red *canali*
Sunday afternoon in paradise
not like my region Lazio
where the afternoons are like fire
they take your breath away
the air in this town is elegant
it deserves to be taken
in small sips
like their wine

i would have loved to take
a bottle back to my grandfather
he had such respect for the
grapevine

Stealing Persimmons

SCENES FROM A BAY WINDOW

Rosa sits by the bay window staring out at the seasons, watching them play like grandchildren. Games played without fear. She watches from dawn till the light dies. Beyond the clump of summer iris, behind the naked crab-apple tree. The games of sunshine. The games of snow. She watches time pass quickly and slowly. She understands time. She knows the minutes of the hour, the hours of the day. She is intimate with time.

Her body is slight, angular. A Modigliani woman in black. It is a color she has come to love, the way she loved her skin before recognizing its roughness, its thirst. Rosa is comfortable here, in this chair with the high, strong back. The wool blanket over her knees and the beads between her fingers. They too are black, coordinated. Her fingers move rapidly. They have resisted well; they defy time. Their energy is outside of her, almost a miracle. Her once soft grey eyes are thick with cataracts. They fog her images. She blinks constantly to focus. The fourth blink, and she is in a field. An open, vast, green pasture surrounded by gentle hills. She traces their shape, their beautiful curves with her finger. Everywhere she runs. She climbs planting her feet like giant seeds in the warm earth. She is breathing in everything with a lustful appetite. All around her the echo of her laughter, a sweet symphony.

In the distance she sees Tomaso. Torn wool pants and an old stained jacket. Always buttons missing. Tomaso's thick small hands scratching the crop of matted black hair. His voice clear as the Sunday bells. '*Corri, Rosa, corri*. I'll meet you at the walnut tree.' He always gets there first. Like two quick lizards they climb the tree. They gather green walnut balls, counting them, throwing them, using them as marbles. And the sweet symphony plays on.

'*Le mucche*. Tomaso, you have to bring the cows back.' They march along, pockets full of walnuts, leading the cows home as the sun settles itself over the scattered hills.

The bay window is her world. It is her memory. At this moment she would like to sleep for a while. Her cloudy eyes hurt, they burn but they will not close. It is as if the lids were sewn to her forehead. She sees Tomaso again. He is in the barn. The October air is cool. It makes her dark skin tingle. 'Get the pail, Rosa.' Tomaso calms the cows. He is gentle and Rosa is always amazed by this. Tomaso's stalky, rough body, his tattered clothes and reckless hair are so unlike his tender manner. He pulls the stool over to sit beneath the heavy teats of the cows and with his small hands begins to pull at their long pink mass. The milk hits the pail like small stones. Like hail on tin rooftops. Rosa leans by the door watching the rhythm of his hands, listening to his whistling as the frothy white foam fills the pail. She turns away, slowly her feet find their way toward the farmhouse.

The clicking of the doorknob and Rosa blinks again. Maria is home. Rosa breathes a small sigh as she watches her daughter throw her bag on the couch and fling her shoes in the corner. '*Ciao, mamma, come stai?*' The response is one Maria knows too well. A frugal smile, a slight bow of the head. Maria understands. She rests her hand on her mother's fingers. A kiss to the forehead and walks away.

Her voice. Why her voice? Rosa thinks. Why not her eyes? She could still see without her eyes. But this cruel, cruel silence.

Tomaso is whistling. The tune is lively, crisp as the autumn leaves flirting outside the window. '*Vieni*, Rosa, let's light the fire before ma and pa get home, it's getting cold.' She gathers and armful of hay and loose bits of wood scooped into her apron. She places them carefully in the stone fireplace and strikes a long, wooden match watching the flames ignite and light up the bare, uneven walls. Soon the kitchen is warm. Soft shadows fluttering around them like thin voiceless birds. They sit, knees beneath their chins, their hands stretched towards the blue-tipped flames.

'Would you like some soup tonight, mamma?' Maria's voice is young. Her little girl's voice. It has not changed much. Rosa moves her head to look at her daughter's face, she nods. Maria understands. It seems they have come to this now. Understanding. No more long conversations. No more stories. No more songs in any language.

Just an understanding of needs. Maria has gone to the kitchen.

Rosa turns to the bay window. Tomaso is shoveling potatoes deep into the ashes of the fireplace. 'We need salt, Rosa.' She lifts the heavy wooden top of a chest, opens a brown bag and scoops out a spoonful of salt. The potatoes open and smoke while Tomaso sprinkles the coarse granules over them. '*Mangia, Rosa, sono buone.*'

'I met an old friend of yours at Nicario's store today, mamma.' Maria speaks as she sets the two plates and glasses on the dining room table. "She said she was from Montecalmo. Her name is Teresa Bovina.' Rosa's fingers stop. Her head turns away from the bay window. 'She told me you stole persimmons together back home in Montecalmo.' Maria's eyes smile. She begins to giggle like a small child. 'Not you, mamma, a thief? I wish you could tell me that story, mamma, I'd love to hear that story.'

This time Rosa's eyes are moist. It takes more than four blinks, but she is there. There with Teresa. They are young, lean, fresh faced and always hungry. They are playing a game, running, leaping over each other like frogs. '*Uno, due, tre, prima io e dopo te, corri, matta.*' They chant silly rhymes as their voices pant with energy. Teresa's is deep like a man's. She is tall and large with a strong, square face. Rosa admires the strength, the confidence in Teresa's laugh. Breathless and laughing, they

44

take air in with large gulps, their cheeks bright pink from the rushing blood and the autumn chill. 'We've got to jump over the fence, Rosa. Look at the persimmons they are so ripe. Come on.' Rosa is always reluctant. He will catch them, Armando will, and he'll chase them with a pitchfork. If he catches them, they will feel the stinging leather of his belt. 'Come on, Rosa. Don't be so afraid, we'll fill our aprons and run. The old mule is too slow he'll never catch us. *Dai, dai andiamo...* Come on.' Teresa is fearless, and Rosa wants to know that feeling. A smile, a wink, and they are hand in hand, like secret sisters. Their long skirts tucked into their waists, lifting their quick strong legs they disappear over the fence.

'Is it true, mamma, did you and Teresa really steal persimmons together?' Maria is back in the room, her tongue tasting a wooden spoon. 'She laughed so hard when she told me about it, I understood it must be a special memory.' Maria walks toward her mother and sits facing her. 'Are you all right, mamma? Look at me.' Rosa lifts her face and looks at Maria. 'Teresa wants to visit you. I told her it would be all right. I thought it might cheer you up to see an old friend. You don't see many anymore.' Rosa turns again to the bay window. Maria remembers the soup and walks towards the kitchen.

They are sitting beneath the walnut tree. The evening air is biting and Teresa wraps her shawl around her shoulders tucking her body close to Rosa's. They are like two schoolgirls exchanging secrets as the sweet orange flesh of persimmon drips from their open lips making sticky little rivers down their chins. They are beneath an evening sky that is a deep, flat purple. Lights begin to dot the countryside like the first fireflies on a summer night. In the distance Tomaso is loading hay onto the wheelbarrow, fresh bedding for the cows. She must get home. 'Why are you always in a hurry?' Teresa complains. 'You little scared *ladra*, one more persimmon before you go.' They laugh and eat huddled together beneath the walnut tree till the chilly night coughs up a giant moon.

Rosa has not seen Teresa in years. Long before this silence, before the pictures from the bay window. She is not sure she wants to see her again. She does not need to see her.

'It's ready, mamma.' Maria walks over wiping her hands onto the cotton apron she always wears when she prepares dinner. 'Let me help you.' Maria takes the beads from her mother's hands placing them on the couch. She folds the blanket and places it beside the beads. She slips her hand under her mother's elbow and gently lifts her to her feet. Maria wraps her other arm around Rosa's delicate body. They take long, slow steps from the window into the dining room. Seven steps. Rosa counts them each time. They sit facing each other. The long teak table covered by a colorful linen tablecloth. Maria has lit some candles. Rosa likes candlelight, it brings back the shadows. They eat in silence. Rosa's spoonfuls take time to reach her thin, pale lips. 'You don't think it's a good idea for Teresa to visit, do you, mamma?' Maria breaks the silence, holding her spoon midway between her mouth and the dish. 'I really think you should have visitors. You are always sitting by the window, staring. You don't see

46

anyone until I come home at night, it must be so lonely for you. Please, mamma, let Teresa come, I know you would enjoy it.' Maria is genuinely concerned and Rosa understands this. In her heart she wants to tell her daughter that she is not alone, she is not lonely. She does not need visitors. But she sees the pain on Maria's face. She does not want pain for her daughter. Her whole life she has tried to shelter her children from pain. It had never occurred to her that perhaps one day Maria's life would come to this. The guardian angel with the face of pain. A dutiful daughter, a nurse. There is anger in Rosa's eyes. Anger at growing old, helpless.

Dinner is over. Maria walks her mother back to the chair by the window. 'Do you want me to turn on the television for a while, mamma, while I do the dishes?' Rosa shakes her head. She does not need television.

The dark comes quickly in late October. The speeding headlights hit the bay window, like shooting stars. Rosa's eyes look up to catch their glowing light. Vito's face is there. His beautiful face. He is standing by the large stone pillar of the church of Saint Anna, under the one light of the piazza and a thousand stars nailed to the clear night sky. Vito's wavy hair is black. A thin mustache, even and neat, beneath a straight strong nose. He is leaning smoking a cigarette, blowing feathery circles that rise like miniature clouds. This beautiful, young man in a city suit wearing shoes that shine. How elegant he looks. Rosa thinks. Not at all like her brother Tomaso. Not at all like the other boys of the town. She feels something strange inside her, in her throat, her stomach, between her thighs. She knows she wants to touch him. She wants to run her hand along his beautiful cheeks. But she stands petrified like the saints in the church.

'I'll make some espresso, mamma, light, so you can sleep.' Maria is calling from the kitchen. Rosa smiles. 'No milk for you right, mamma?' Her eyes close. When they open again she is at the dining room table. The children are all there. Marco, Concetta, Mimma the oldest and little Maria. 'We want coffee too, mamma, with milk and lots and lots of sugar.' There is always an argument. 'You are all too little for coffee, it's not good for you.' The children protest. 'Yes, it is, mamma, yes, it is.' They always win.

'Coffee is ready, mamma. Mamma, were you daydreaming again?' Rosa turns to look at Maria, watching her stir the tiny cups with a tinier spoon. Maria hands Rosa the coffee. They sit in silence. They do not need words. Perhaps everything has already been said. Perhaps words are only an ornament. They sit for a long time, breathing, sipping coffee. They are one large shadow on the living room wall. 'I bet you were off stealing persimmons again, hey, mamma?'

'I'm going to take a bath, mamma.' Maria stands and walks away. Rosa counts the footsteps up the creaky stairs. All sounds seem sharper now. Once, sounds were something to avoid. The sounds of her loud children growing up. The sounds of the factory machines bouncing from hard walls without windows. The sound of her husband's serious, humorless voice. She had often sheltered herself from sounds. But now all sounds were welcome, all sounds lost friends.

Her eyes on the bay window and he is there again. Vito was her first love, her only real love. 'You must come with me, Rosa. There is nothing here for you, for us. Nothing for anyone in this town.' The sound of Vito's clear voice. His hands firm on her arms. The blood has stopped. He is shaking her, wanting her to understand, to accept his dream. Rosa stares into his huge eyes. She recognizes the passion and the fear. She envies his eyes. 'I cannot leave them. I cannot go with you, they need me here.' She feels her heart rebel inside her chest, wanting to reach the words escaping from her throat, to choke them. She walks away, watching the night swallow his face, his beautiful face, the sound of his voice, forever.

'The bath was wonderful, mamma. It feels good to be clean.' Maria is wrapped in her white robe with the red dots. She comes to sit by Rosa straightening the blanket on her mother's knees. 'You know, Teresa, she told me that you almost married another man before you met papa. Oh how I wish you could tell me that story, mamma.' They both smile and turn their heads toward the bay window.

There is no real reason for stories now, no real need for them, why trouble Maria with more. At times, Rosa wishes her other children would unburden Maria for a while. But their lives are so full of everyday things. The way her own life had once been. She hopes Maria understands.

'I was thinking, mamma, it might be nice to take a trip to Montecalmo this coming summer. What do you think?' Maria's dark eyes widen with possibilities. She stares at her mother hoping for a response. A positive response. 'I would love to see all the places you used to tell us about. The farmhouse you lived in, the hills you and uncle Tomaso climbed, the persimmon trees. I think it would be good for you and for me.' Rosa sees the excitement in her daughter's face. She wants to hold her in her arms. She wants to tell her one last story. 'No, Maria, those places are not there anymore. Look, Maria. Look out the window. There's Tomaso trying to juggle the walnut balls. He's not very good. Keeps dropping them. Look, Maria. There I am. It has started to rain. I must put the pails out to catch the rainwater. Look at me run, Maria, look how fast I can run.' A quick shooting star from the bay window lights up the room. They look at each other, understanding something new. Maria wraps her arms around her mother's shoulders, letting her hands rest on Rosa's beating chest. They are again one large shadow, gently rocking. 'You know, mamma, tomorrow when I go by Mr. Nicario's store I'm going to steal a couple of sweet, ripe persimmons for me and you.'

The Bride's Return

ANTONIETTA

The red hot Sicilian sun
will not wait
one day is all he has left
silent
on his mother's best sheets
on the pale cotton blanket
she crocheted with the last
light of her eyes
the African breath from
across the ocean
will not allow much more time
for sleeping

the women in black
in the month of July
they sit around his still body
wailing in chorus
quick fingers fondling
the smooth pebbles of rosary beads
while the men
solemn
in their arm bands and buttons
stand like dark pillars
around the crowded room

the children's nervous laughter
spilling and scattering
like large stones in the hard

corners of the courtyard
his young bride is on a train
Rome to Sicily, 1948
it is a long, slow trip
the young bride has eyes
the color of walnuts
they settle over the countryside
and through sleepy lids
they glimpse the lazy hills
and the endless parade
of wide umbrella pines

she will meet the procession
when her journey ends
she will swallow the thick
scent of chrysanthemums
and gasp for air
she will not love him again

she will remember forever
the hot Sicilian sun with
its cruel, open grin

Ode to Balls

I could say his ego is the size
of Los Angeles
but that would be kind
let me speak of his genitals

he was always admiring his
in mirrors, shiny tiles on bathroom walls
even the toaster when it was strategically placed
i often moved the espresso pot out of his way
they were everywhere
i bumped into them from across the room
i found them in open drawers or lounging
romantically on the balcony floor
how he loved them
he could not do enough for them
he wrote them poems
and played music for them
John Denver records
he photographed them in color
and in black and white
and lit perfumed candles on summer nights
i believe he's left them everything in his will
on Saturday nights
he dressed them up and took them dancing
how he loved them
they weren't fat
they weren't loud
they weren't awkward
they were graceful
they danced into the room

and the world stopped

i could say his ego is the size
of Los Angeles but
that would be kind

Winters

How short the winters have become
January is no longer the enemy
this season she dreaded
like the magnolia dreads the
first, cruel breath of wind
this season is so much tamer now
perhaps she fools herself
in thinking the years are kinder
but time moves so much faster now,
too fast to linger in the dream
too fast to dine slowly

she has put away the fur coat
it is no longer *correct* or needed
no time to clean out the summer closet
or the winter closet, they have become one
in harmony with each other's dust
even the birds outside her window
refuse to fly away
they make do on her stale bread
dipped in red wine
they too should feast
the snow melts so
quickly

The Last Season

MARISA

Which season do i ask for
one more summer
to plant the seeds
to watch my garden grow
to dig up the fig tree my father
left behind
to watch the sun drape itself
around the trees
the way my grandmother draped her
shawl around me
one more summer to watch my
children's changing bodies
their beautiful skin exposed

do i ask you for autumn
i am fond of autumn
of the taste of crisp apples
how much time is enough time
the seasons are too short
and now my life is measured by
just one more
and i am not ready to die
so i pray all the prayers i have learned
i kiss all the relics and cross myself
with holy water
i sleep with the pictures of saints
with the stigmata of Padre Pio
in between the pillow case

my friends sit around me and talk
of the past
they are here to help me
i accommodate them
they are sincere
but i want the future
i want the seasons over and over
i want to be at my childrens' wedding
i am not afraid, God
i am just not ready

Lesson: The Next Hello

To Marisa

Death halves us:
every loss
divides
our narrowness
and we are less.

Dorothy Livesay

I

What do i learn from this
there must be something
to learn
all things have reasons
death is and is not
a subject for poetry
time is no time
our children become motherless
with or without prayers
cancer is real
your skin is a color
without a name
your eyes no longer clear
your smile forced from pain
or fear
i touch your hand and it is cold
your steps are slow, more like strides
you sleep long hours, the morphene
controlling your pain
i learn that i am helpless
as i pour ice water to cool
your burning throat

II

i watched you sleep for hours today
just you and me
i could not disturb you
i sat and watched your face change
your lips open
as if air could not find its way in
the oxygen bubbles dancing
completely unaware

III

how difficult to find the words
they seem so senseless
but it is all i have to give you
it is all i have that comes from the
deepest part of me where i protect
beautiful things
it is where you always are
safe, inside where darkness
has no space

you were the magnolia
always first to bloom
breathtaking in its beauty
always first to smile
to suggest the song
to master the dance steps

i loved you for that
you with all the talent
for things i stumbled with
how you tried to teach me
to thread that sewing machine

but i had no patience
you wrote out the recipes
but i always misplaced them

the thousand evenings we spent
together with our flirtatious hearts
incredible dreams that seemed so possible
and so much laughter

i imagined our conversations
would last forever
i imagined us old and wrinkled
with our fingernails still painted red
i imagined us comparing
heartaches again and again
but you could not wait
the way you made me wait
always late for our appointments
as if time had no meaning
or place in your life

i will miss you, sweet friend
you who loved me without conditions
you who opened your heart like a glass door
and made room for everyone
and asked little in return
but you were given the world
and knew it
Joseph, Joey, Sandra and Lucas
such blessings, such love
no riches can measure

i look into your mother's eyes
and see you
i listen to your brother's voice

and hear you
you are in our hearts
every other beat
for you

i will not say good-bye
there are no good-byes
between friends
just long, long silences
until the next hello

Ladies of the Caravelle

The photographs are all
black and white
young, olive skinned women
with thick hair piled neatly
at the back of the neck
or cut short in tight curls

i recognize the coral beads
not quite pearls
my own grandmother wore four strings
of them around her neck
my older cousins were fortunate
in their inheritance
and have used the beads to fashion
earrings, pins and other decorative things

the smiles never reveal the teeth
they are smiles for photographs
the hands poised uncomfortably
on someone's shoulder
or the back of a chair

sometimes they are holding
something awkward
something that seems not to belong
a pair of lace gloves that were never worn
a crystal glass
or a bouquet of perfect flowers

their skin is flawless

they are all beautiful
beautiful with being young
beautiful with being photographed

i sit with them on Saturday afternoons
at the long table they have filled
with home made *biscotti* and *ciambelle*
they show me each photograph
with so much pride
and with each one there is a story
a story of a town
a story of a man
a story of a wedding
a story of a death
and with each one there is a
song in dialect i understand

we arrange the photographs neatly
on bristol board paper and label
the year, the region, the date of departure
the port of embarkment, the date of arrival
and then the names: Maria, Concetta,
Adele, Rina, Rosa, Speranza

the photographs will be on display
in the lobby of a building
where strangers will come
to view them, to interpret their history
their cultural elegance

strangers will not hear the
songs in dialect
the women packaged them for me
to take home with the leftover *ciambelle*
and *biscotti*

My Father's Cane

I sit on the cement stoop
below my father's black
and white photograph
the one he used the last time
for his passport
the date of his birth and death
in clear print
on a smoky, square marble
the white magnolia's petals
scattered like giant communion wafers
on the soft waking earth
the birds do their silent dance
balancing on the gravestones
the trees wear their green
like a new haircut

it is a magic afternoon
the kind we pray for
and hunger for each time
this season decides to
tease us again
my father's cane beside me
it is what he left me
that is practical
i use it when my back
refuses to hold me
it accompanies me
when i visit
on special occasions

Christmas, Easter
when nostalgia and guilt
invade my heart
i have little to say to him now
thirteen years since we ended
the argument
i no longer rely on the anger
i justified with youth
his cane in my hand
and i understand his steps
the weight of his legs
the wounds in his heart
this place i come to
rarely
gives me back my father
the one i wanted in my life
the one who loved me
the way i wanted to be loved

perhaps it is the season
that forgives
that refuses to judge
i know here
beneath this blue sky
with my feet on the earth
i let the tears flow
without shame
without fear
i hear them being swallowed
deep into the white silence
of my father's bones
his dry bones
that have no more need
for his cane

A Mother Poem

LUCIANA

I

Mamma had no time to baby me
after her breasts emptied
my father packed his one suitcase
and crossed the ocean to prepare
a new life for all of us
he hung his blue jacket
on the nail by the door
its pockets empty of chocolates

mamma took a job at the local hospital
long hours, midnight shifts, Sundays
she held the hands of the dying old
and wiped the blood of premature mothers
she boiled the instruments and learned
to give advice
and every other afternoon she biked
for miles from town to town
injecting needles in *contadini*

mamma had no time for playgrounds
she left me in the Catholic arms
of Sister Bernarda and Sister Plaudilla
whose small dry breasts were resting places
for large crucifixes, no room there for
small faces with wet eyes

mamma thought i was in good hands
safe hands, what better hands than
those of the sacred and divine
she knew nothing of the darkness
of the medieval tower, she only
ever saw the large *portone*
and the waiting room
where the nuns brought me down for visits
all starched, combed and clean

mamma fed me *ricotta* and *maritozzi*
and in between kisses i could hear
her heart snap like a dry crust of bread
i could feel her body shake each time
she put her arms around me
and whispered good-bye
my screams didn't convince her to turn back
i watched her walk away toward the hospital
her sky blue sweater on her shoulders
her tight curls stiff as her footsteps
mamma never turned around

II

my baby wears Nikes
and little Gap shirts
she's full of authors
magic, music and Raffi
she's in love with parks
and Canada's Wonderland
i'm my baby's personal driver
i'm her immediate cash drawer
sometimes she remembers i'm there
and says, 'I love you, mommy, can
we go to McDonalds?'

III

when i was eight
Sister Bernarda made me a pallbearer
a little white casket
on six little shoulders
our steps controlled and careful
over the cobblestones

IV

my baby is scared of ghosts
and only wants stories with happy endings
sometimes i sneak a story
that makes her cry
then my baby looks like me

V

mamma takes her in her arms
and fills her with kisses and
chocolate bars
trying to buy back a little bit of time
mamma does not want to hear my baby cry
my baby calls her name and mamma always
turns around

Changes

I watch my mother's face change
i watch her body move with careful steps
no longer confident
as if her feet were strangers
her shoes have lost the height of youth
i listen to her words always
punctuated with a sigh
of relief or resignation
she sits longer in the chair eating
she lies longer in her bed sleeping
the dishes often wait

i want to believe she is
now doing all the things
she had no time for
the things that require plenty
of time, a gift of retirement
of grown children and dead husbands
this woman who ran everywhere
and whose eyes opened before the
sky did, before the sun did
this woman who never sat for a meal
but ate standing as she choreographed
the serving of everyone

i watch my mother and i see
my face change
i recognize the shape of my body
she looks at my child and sees
me

I Might Have Been Sicilian

GIACINTA

If her first husband had lived
i might have been Sicilian
i might have learned to swim
in the blue waters of the Ionian
i might have been less tall
my hair a different color
my dialect less musical
i might have felt the scirocco
from Northern Africa
and climbed tangerine trees
but he died while his young bride
spoke to her sisters about her
new life, not in Canada but Catania
he died while his bride
sat beneath the Roman pines
speaking of the gentle husband
who bought her dresses that
swung in perfect circles
he died while the accordion
played a love song to Donna Rosa
as she freed her braids to
the summer moon
if he had lived long enough
to give her children
i might have been Sicilian

Compagno

I am a married woman
i am a mother
i recognize myself
in these things

they define me
they show me where to sit
and when to stand
but you still love me

and it does not concern you
that i am a married woman
that i am a mother
this is not a problem for you

your eyes look at me
you speak my name
and English is a forgotten
language
you and i have no need
for language

your eyes are wide open
but you do not see the changes
my hair in different shades
the way my laughter looks for reasons
you don't notice the pause
between my thoughts
the earlier departure
from the *caffè* table

the need for sleep
the bedtime stories
that must be read

you do not see the me
that i have become and
for this i return each time
with more years in my suitcase
i come back to you
i come back to me

Loreta, la calda

They won't talk about sex
they talk about everything else

it embarrasses them
as if their children
were all announcements by Gabriel
you know, the Angel

not me, it doesn't embarrass me
i had my legs wide open
as well as my eyes
look at their faces
they hide them
red with shame
for having desires

not me, i felt my man
and he felt me
i was so beautiful
non sapeva dove metterlo

you think i am vulgar
i talk vulgar
an old woman shouldn't
talk so vulgar

but i wasn't always old
only death is old
only death is vulgar

Cuore

EMILIA AND ANTONIO

I have taken my heart
to so many places
like Hansel and Gretel
in the dark of the forest
i left bits and pieces
pebbles of light
to find my way back
back to my father's house
where the lamp is dim
but always lit
back to where my friends live
where there is always a chair
for me and a full glass of wine
back to re-arrange my clothes
my boxes of photographs
then again i take my heart
to the next place
where it is home for a while
a little less heavy than before
but alone with itself
until one autumn afternoon
when the wind forced its way
into my open chest
and i stumbled into you
a pebble in a canyon
a seed in an endless field
just one single note
to complete the symphony

i have taken my heart
to so many places
but now it will not move
anywhere
without
you

Ultimo Tango con Neruda

Per Massimo Troisi

The woman in Pablo's arms
the dark one he twirls
like a pinwheel
so effortlessly
in the cool of an oleander night
as the sky opens its shutters
to dust out a tablecloth full
of half-eaten stars

that woman
is a metaphor
you and Pablo spit out
like melon pits
and the grappa goes down
smooth
on long summer nights

one last tango
on a rose-stained terrazza
a poet and a clown
two hearts so large
the world can only take
the weight of one
when the dance is over
you will be gone
leaving us the tune
the steps the metaphor

Perfect Love

He left me for a girl
who drove a beige Subaru

he left me for a girl
whose breasts didn't need a bra

he left me for a girl
whose smooth white thighs
opened without guilt

he left me for a girl
who didn't need confession
who didn't hang rosary beads
on bedroom walls

he left me for a girl
whose blood was bluer than her eyes

he left me for a girl
whose accent was charmingly English

he left me for a love
that wouldn't confuse him
a love that was perfect

she left him
for someone with a
bigger car

A Poet

*if you're not living on the edge
you're taking up too much room*
Len Gasparini

His voice can take you anywhere
even places you'll never want to go
he's been there and he lets you know it
with the sly, slow turn of his tongue
as the giant hand smooths the hair
left on his powerful, handsome head
the profile fit for a coin

twenty years ago i first heard him
deliver his poems
the Sicilian from Windsor, Detroit,
Montreal, Louisiana
the poet for the mafia
the women in the room all wanting him
the men in the room all wanting to be him
i was never quite sure what he wanted
but four wives later
he's still looking for home

between the whores and the highways
neon lights and angels
he drops poems along the way
they explode into flames
beacons of light for his way back
or maybe not

Donna/Woman

Only when a woman is
nothing
but a dream he believes
when she walks on his heart
like a ghost
who brings back his identity
the history they stole
when they bundled him up
and took him away

only a dark woman
without a voice
a dark woman whose eyes
are his
only when a woman is nothing
but a muse
a subject to write about
an angel, a witch
whose sweet poison he drinks
to remember
to be
to write
and when a woman is only
this
can she be killed so easily
in the name of love

Sometimes She Hates Her Poems

She has used her poems
as an excuse
always as a reason
for her lack of courage
for her anti-social behavior
she has used them to explain
the laziness of her body
the vacuum of her spirit
artists are allowed to be capricious
but she is not proud of this

sometimes she hates her poems
what they reveal of her

she wants to dream averageness
dream of loving the routines of life
of recognizing the importance of laundry
and forgetting metaphors
she dreams of dusting furniture happily
and having long conversations over coffee
about balloon curtains, about the desire to
purchase a piece of clothing by Versace or Klein
she would like to buy *Cosmopolitan*
and take its tests
on how to be a good lover or mother
on how to increase whatever appetite
sometimes she dreams the peacefulness of stupidity
the liberation that comes from an ignorant heart

Parts of Her

GIOVANNA

Her sun porch window
her desk
her old Olivetti
and her hands
the light at her window
intrudes
comes to tell her
something
creeping in
between the beige
of the venetian blind
her plastic armor
against the world
she rises
and walks away
with the sharp bite
in her knees
a pain she begrudged
her father
when she was restless and
foolish
she walks by the kitchen mirror
and notices her face
she pulls back the hair
her face still confusing
the lids above the eye
no longer take the
shadow smoothly

her lips outlined by a
colored pencil
she lifts her hand
and slides it under
her second chin
her hand is so large
she raises the other one
together they are frightening
but they speak to her louder
than her two languages
they are volumes of poetry
she knows herself
by these hands
these hands on her face
on her furniture
on her husband's body
on her child's sleeping eyes
these hands that still hold the pen
to shape letters into words

if only she knew her heart
as well as her hands know
their responsibility